Thomas Tomkins
Musician, Citizen, Victim of War

Thomas Tomkins
Musician, Citizen, Victim of War

By Revd. Canon Paul Tongue

First published in Great Britain in 2012 by
The Battle of Worcester Society
The Commandery
Sidbury
Worcester
WR1 2HU

Copyright © Paul Tongue 2012

ISBN: 978-0-9572421-0-4

The right of Paul Tongue to be identified as Author of the work has been asserted by him in accordance with the Copyright, Designs, and Patents Act 1988.

All rights reserved. No part of this book may be reproduced of transmitted in any form or by any means, electronic or mechanical including photocopying, recording or by any information storage and retrieval system, without permission from the publisher in writing.

All images appear courtesy of the Worcester Cathedral Library and are available for first hand perusal by appointment. The Battle of Worcester Society would like to extend its thanks to Worcester Cathedral for its assistance with this publication.

For a complete list of publications please contact

THE BATTLE OF WORCESTER SOCIETY
The Commandery, Sidbury, Worcester, WR1 2HU
Email: publishing@thebattleofworcestersociety.org.uk
Website: www.thebattleofworcestersociety.org.uk

CONTENTS

The Battle of Worcester Society..i

Revd Canon Paul Tongue...ii

Thomas Tomkins' *(Senior)* Immediate Family Tree................................1

His Parents and Family..2

Thomas Number Two...4

The Dallam Organ..6

Gentleman of the Chapel Royal..14

Thomas and Alice - Citizens and Benefactors......................................16

Civil War...19

The Final Years...23

Postmortem..24

IMAGES

All images appear courtesy of the Worcester Cathedral Library.
The Worcester Cathedral Library has been an integral part of the life of Worcester Cathedral since Anglo-Saxon times. It exists to facilitate research by scholars. It is a resource for cathedral staff carrying out repair work on the building, and for relevant local and family history enquiries by members of the public, and through tours for interested groups, the library enables ordinary people to see historic books and ancient documents.
Thanks go to David Morrison (Cathedral Librarian) for his time and assistance in compiling the images contained within this work.
The images are reproduced here by permission of the Chapter of Worcester Cathedral (U.K.).

For further information please email;
info@worcestercathedral.org.uk

The Battle of Worcester Society

The Battle of Worcester 1651 was the final battle of the English Civil Wars and is regarded as one of the most significant battles to have occurred on English soil. Not only did it change the course of political, social and religious history in this country but other countries across the globe also felt its ramifications.

In 1786 two of the most important Americans in history visited Worcester and saw sights associated with the battle. They were John Adams and Thomas Jefferson. John Adams was to become the second President of the United States of America and Thomas Jefferson the third. They were two of the founding forefathers and took their lead from the Battle of Worcester 1651. On the subject of Worcester Adams wrote in his diary;

"And do Englishmen so soon forget the ground where liberty was fought for? Tell your neighbours and your children that this is holy ground, much holier than that on which your churches stand. All England should come in pilgrimage to this hill once a year."

The BoWS agrees with John Adams. Our mandate includes campaigning for a suitable monument to the thousands of men that died that day,

The Battle of Worcester Society endeavours to publish material relating to the Civil War and its causes and affects. Our publications include
The Black Pear Journal, a quarterly journal for the members of the society as well as the general public. The journal contains articles from historians as well as anything of interest to the society.

The Revd. Canon Paul Tongue

Paul Tongue was born in Worcester and educated at Worcester Royal Grammar School. He studied Theology and trained for the Priesthood at St Chad's College, Durham University (1959 -64), graduating with an Honours Degree in Theology (1963) and a Diploma in Theology (1964). After Ordination he served the whole of his ministry in the Black Country.

He served his title at St. Edmund's Church, Dudley (1964-69), and a second curacy at St. Andrew, The Straits, in the Parish of All Saints, Sedgley (1969-70). In 1970 he became Vicar of Holy Trinity, Amblecote, Stourbridge, where he remained until his retirement in 2007. In 1994 he was made an Honorary Canon of Worcester Cathedral. From 1996-2002 he served as Rural Dean of Stourbridge.

In retirement he became a regular worshipper at Worcester Cathedral, having moved to his family home nearby. He also became involved with the Worcester City Branch of the Royal British Legion. In 2009 he researched and presented an Exhibition in the Cathedral to mark the 80th Anniversary of the death of Geoffrey Studdert Kennedy, better known by his nickname 'Woodbine Willie', arguably the most famous of all the Army Chaplains in the First World War.

Since 2008 he has officiated at Drumhead Services with the Battle of Worcester Society. In 2011 he devised and led a service in the Cathedral marking the 360th Anniversary of the Battle of Worcester. Since 2010 he has served as Honorary Succentor at Worcester Cathedral, singing Evensong at most of the Services. This involvement with the music of the Cathedral has brought about his interest in Thomas Tomkins, the longest serving Organist in the life of the Cathedral. This book brings together his dual interests in the music of the Cathedral and the Civil War.

Immediate Family Tree of Thomas Tomkins

A   **Thomas Tomkins**
(Senior)
1st Family

Thomas Tomkins *(Senior)* —m— Margaret Tomkins

- Thomas Tomkins
- Bridget Tomkins
- **Thomas Tomkins** b. 1572 — Alice Patrick b. 1563
  - Nathaniel Thomas b. 1599

B   **Thomas Tomkins**
(Senior)
2nd Family

Thomas Tomkins *(Senior)* —m— Anne Hargest

- John — m — Margaret
  - John
  - Sylvanus
  - Thomas
- Robert
- Nicholas
- Giles
- Peregrine
- Margaret
- Elizabeth

The focus of this book is Thomas Tomkins who is show on chart A in bold and born in 1572.

The purpose of this simple family tree is to illustrate the family connections referred to in this work and should not be considered a genealogical reference.
E.g. Thomas Tomkins (b. 1572) may well have had many other half nephews and nieces but only the three shown here are referred to in this book.

HIS PARENTS AND FAMILY

In 1565 Thomas Tomkins senior, father of Thomas Tomkins, Organist and Master of Choristers at Worcester from 1596 to 1654, left his home in Lostwithiel, in Cornwall, with Margaret his wife, and Thomas, their first born, to take up the position of Vicar Choral at St David's Cathedral in Wales. They set up home, and soon a second child Bridget was born. However, rather confusingly their first born, Thomas is not the subject of this book. (All will be revealed!) The marriage was not smooth, and in 1571 Margaret returned to Cornwall and Thomas senior was hauled over the coals by the Dean and Chapter of St David's for an extramarital affair with a maidservant. They obviously valued his services highly, because he retained his position, on promising to make amends for his misdemeanour. Margaret returned to St David's and in the following year another child was born. He also, rather confusingly, was named Thomas. There is much speculation that this Thomas, whose story we tell, was the love child of his father and his Welsh maidservant.

Life continued for the family, and Thomas senior was well thought of by the Dean and Chapter of St David's, so much so that he was appointed Master of Choristers and Organist in 1577. However, sometime before 1586 Margaret died and Thomas senior re-married in 1586. His second wife was Anne Hargest, the daughter of a local farmer near St David's. Thomas was unhappy with his stipend, and found a new position as a Minor Canon at Gloucester Cathedral, where both he and Anne were to stay until their deaths. Thomas and Anne had seven children: John, Robert, Nicholas, Giles, Peregrine, Margaret, and Elizabeth. John was to become Organist at King's College, Cambridge, and then Organist at St Paul's Cathedral, London, and a member of the Chapel Royal. Robert was to become a talented Viol player in the King's Musick. Giles followed John as Organist at King's College, Cambridge and then became Organist at Salisbury Cathedral. No wonder Charles Burney, in his General History of Music, published in 1776, wrote: "The Tomkins family produced more able musicians during the sixteenth and seventeenth centuries than any other which England can boast."

Meanwhile Thomas Number 1, Thomas senior's first born, had joined the Royal Navy. In 1588 he died on board HMS Revenge during action against 53 Spanish ships. As the years went by Thomas senior was appointed Incumbent variously at Tredington, near Tewkesbury, and two livings in the City of Gloucester to finance his growing family. In 1605 he was appointed Canon Precentor at Gloucester Cathedral.

THOMAS NUMBER TWO

We tell the story of his son Thomas, born at St David's in 1572. Despite his father's extramarital affair he was brought up by Margaret, and always spoke of her as his mother. He became a pupil of the most famous of all Elizabethan musicians, William Byrd. Much later in life he was to dedicate one of his compositions "To my ancient and much reverenced master William Byrd". It seems probable that he studied with him in his late teens in London, and may then have lived in Worcester from 1593 with a relative, the wealthy clothier John Tomkins. It is certain that in 1593 he began a non-residential course with Magdalen College, Oxford, which was to last fourteen years until he graduated with a degree of Bachelor of Music in 1607.

In the mean time he was appointed Organist and Master of the Choristers at Worcester Cathedral in 1596 at the age of 24 years. The annual pay was £11. 6s 8d. He succeeded Nathaniel Patrick who died the previous year, the same year in which his only child also died. Nathaniel's widow went back to her family at Longdon, near Tewkesbury. Whether Thomas already knew her we do not know, but a year after his appointment to Worcester Thomas married Nathaniel's widow Alice. They were married at Tewkesbury Abbey on the 24th May, 1597; he was 25 and she 34 years old. She came back to her former house on College Green, in Worcester, a house which doubled up as the Cathedral Song School. It is the house No 2, but it included half of what is now No 3. It was there that two years later their only child was born. He was named Nathaniel after Alice's first husband, Nathaniel Patrick.

Already Thomas was making a name for himself in the musical world of his day. After the death of Queen Elizabeth I he wrote a 7 part anthem for the Coronation of King James I in 1603. "Be strong and of good courage". He was already known in London, where he had studied under William Byrd as a teenager and up to the age of 21. In 1601, in 'The triumphs of Oriana', edited by Thomas Morley, he had written one piece: 'The Fauns and Satyrs tripping'. But these were turbulent times. In 1604 King James ordered a new translation of the Bible, that was to be published seven years later (the Authorized Version – the King James Bible) In 1605 King James ordered all Roman Catholic priests to leave the country, leading to the Gunpowder Plot.

Worcester City had many Puritan businessmen, and the County was rife with Roman Catholic recusants, both refusing to do their Sunday duty of attending the established Church. Add to this the frequent visits of the Plague, in 1597, 1609, 1610, 1617, 1625, 1630, 1637 (when 1,551 citizens died), 1644 and 1645. The City was very overcrowded. Between 1563 and 1646 the population doubled to 7,000, and Worcester was the 12th largest city in England.

The Organist's House, and Song School (with the white rendering) in which Thomas lived from 1596 -1627

THE DALLAM ORGAN

In 1610 a breath of fresh air came to Worcester in the form of the new Bishop, Henry Parry. He was a great supporter of the arts, and had been one of the prime movers in founding the Bodleian Library in Oxford. He was imbued with vision and an ability to infuse others with his own enthusiasm for worthwhile schemes. He took on board Tomkins great desire to have at Worcester an organ built to his own design, and worthy of his talents. The result was one of Tomkins' greatest contributions to the musical life of the Cathedral – the installation of a new organ, on top of the Choir Screen. The Choir screen had been erected in 1556, five years after the old monastic screen had been demolished. The monastic screen had stood two bays west of the tower in the present Nave near the present Nave Pulpit. The 1556 Screen was in the same position now occupied by the Victorian Screen, immediately to the east of the Crossing. Two small organs had been placed in the North Quire Aisle in 1556, and these were not very satisfactory.

Thomas Dallam was the most famous Organ builder of his day. Towards the end of Queen Elizabeth's reign he had been commissioned to build an Organ as a present from Queen Elizabeth I to the Sultan of Turkey. In 1606 he had built a new organ at King's College Chapel, Cambridge. In 1612 he was commissioned by Arthur Lake, the Dean, to build a new organ for Worcester Cathedral. When the new organ was opened in 1613 it was described as "a magnificent instrument to rival any in the land". It had cost £381. 2s. 8d. – at today's price about £750,000 (not that different to the new organ built in the same Cathedral in 2008 A.D.) 120 people had contributed to the cost, and their arms were blazoned on the case for all to see. It was placed on top of the 1556 Screen at the entrance to the Choir. It was described in 1639, by the antiquary Thomas Habington, like this:

"At the west and highest ascent into the Choir is mounted aloft a most fair and excellent organ adorned with imperial crowns, red roses, including the white fleurs-de-lis, pomegranates, being all Royal badges. Toward the top are two stars, with the one, "H Parry, Episcopus"; with the other, "A Lake, Decanus; and written about the organ: By the meditation and mediation of Thomas Tomkins, Organist here unto the

Righte reverend Bishop and venerable Deane, who gave theise munificent guiftes and invited their fryndes, by the industry of the said Thomas Tomkins".

Bishop Henry Parry and Dean Arthur Lake headed the list of donors, giving £20 each (more than one tenth of the total cost). The organ was in two parts – the Great Organ on the Nave side of the Screen and the Chair Organ on the Quire side of the Screen. The Organist sat between the two on a chair, accompanying the Choir on the Chair organ, and turning round to play the main organ. There were no pedals. It was a century or more later the Chair organ came to be known as the Choir organ, and was integrated with the Great Organ.

18th Century Picture, showing the same Screen, built in 1556, on which the Dallam Organ was installed.

The Benefactors

	li	s	d
The Lo: Bishopp: Parry	20	00	00
The Deane: Lake	20	00	00
The Cittie and Chamber of Worcester	20	00	00
Mr Edward Newport of Hanly	10	00	00
Richard Rice	11	00	00
Sr John Packinton and his Lady	10	00	00
Tho: Lord Windsor	6	13	4
Mr Henry Bromley	6	13	4
Mr William Bromley	6	13	4
Mr Robert Bromley	6	13	4
The Lord Compton	5	0	0
Sr Thomas Lury	5	0	0
Mr Thomas Sevorne of Clares	5	0	0
Mr Ralph Sheldon	5	0	0
Mr William Sebert	5	0	0
Mr Thomas Corbs of Cromly	5	0	0
Mr Humph: Packinton of Chadsley	5	0	0
Mr John Bridges of Eastanton	5	0	0
Sr Edward Pitt	5	0	0
Sr John Alston	4	0	0
Doctor Richard Thornton & his wife	5	0	0
Mr Barksdale and his wife	5	0	0
Sr Edward Blount	4	10	0
Sr Thomas Russell	3	6	8
Mr William Joffs	3	6	0
William Gower	3	0	0
Sr Francis Smith	3	0	0

List of Donors for the Dallam Organ, headed by the Bishop and Dean

	£	s	d
S.r William Sendaud	3	0	0
M.ris Littleton of ffrankley	3	0	0
S.r ffran: Egeoke	3	0	0
S.r William Sands	3	0	0
M.r John Winter	3	0	0
S.r William Walsh & his Lady	3	0	0
Of the Towne of Warwick	3	6	8
M.r Hanbury of London	2	4	0
The Lady Blount of Sillington	2	10	0
D.r John Archbold	2	10	0
S.r Arnold Ligon	2	10	0
S.r Thomas Lucas	2	10	0
S.r Clement Throgmorton	2	10	0
Robert Lee Esq.r	2	10	0
William Cooke Vintner	2	10	0
M.r Thornhill	2	10	0
M.r ffrancis Moore	2	0	0
John Hanford Esq.r	2	0	0
Thomas Russell of Rushock	2	0	0
Anthony Barnes	2	0	0
ffrancis Hirks	2	0	0
Walter Jones	2	0	0
Richard Inglethorp	2	0	0
Thomas Nash	2	0	0
John ffleet	2	0	0

	li	s	d
William Sauage	2	0	0
Francis Sharewell	2	0	0
John Washborn	2	0	0
Sr John Turk	2	0	0
Sr Thomas Beaufo	2	0	0
Mr Dingley	2	0	0
Sr Edmund Wild	2	0	0
Dr Swaldon Clerk deaton	2	0	0
Robert Barnfoild	2	0	0
Nicholas ffortescu	1	13	0
Thomas Countrey	1	10	0
William Richardson	1	10	0
Mr Cooxer of Horick	1	10	0
Leonard Jeffreys	1	10	0
Thomas Cook	1	10	0
Bartholomew Hales	1	10	0
Richard Potter	1	10	0
Thomas Warren	1	10	0
Mr ffrymen	1	10	0
Sr Richard Vernon	1	2	0
Lady Hunks	1	2	0
Sr Richard Grenus	1	2	0
Anthony Langston	1	2	0
William Wenningsty	1	2	0
Thomas Gower of Wick	1	2	0
Mr Cornwall Baron	1	2	0
Dr Helme Chancelr	1	0	0
Mris Throckmorton wid	1	0	0

	li	s	d
Mr Warmstrey Widowe	1	0	0
Charles Stanford	1	0	0
Anthony Skynner	1	0	0
John Rous	1	0	0
John Savage	1	0	0
William Coles	1	0	0
George Sheppard	1	0	0
Edward Barrett	1	0	0
Parson Horton of Fredington	1	0	0
William Corbyn	1	0	0
Henry Ligon	1	0	0
John Wood	1	0	0
Thomas Moore of More	1	0	0
William Ingram	1	0	0
Mr Vernon	1	0	0
John Skinner	1	0	0
Henry Wright	1	0	0
Mr Coxley	0	13	4
Mr Dormoll	0	10	0
William Langston	0	10	0
Henry Langston	0	10	0
Thomas Walsh	0	10	0
Mr Combs	0	10	0
Mr Trinnell	0	10	0
Mrs Margaret Sheldon	0	10	0
William Haine Chandler	0	10	0
Mr Smith of Ripple	0	10	0

M:ris Russell Wid.	0	5	0
M:ris Barnaby	0	5	0
of her Husband	0	2	6
M:r John Combs	0	6	0
A Contribution from Dr Charlet	0	10	0

Anno Dni 1613   D. 248

	£	s	d
All the materialls and workmanshipp of the newe double Organ in the Cathedrall Church of Worcester, to Thomas Dallam organmaker came to	211	00	00
The Case and Joyners worke about the loft to Robert Kettle	68	14	8
The floore and loft in Carpenters worke about	13	00	00
The guilding and painting to William Peacy	77	08	00

The particulars of the great Organ

Two open diapasons of mettall
CC fa ut a pipe of 10 foot long

Two principals of mettal
Two Small principals or 15th of mettal
One twelfth of mettal
One recorder of mettal, a Stopt pipe

In the Chaire Organ

One principal of mettal
One diapason of Wood
One flute of Wood
One Small principal or fifteenth of mettal
One two and twentieth of mettal

July 2, 1666.
Add in ye new organ. An open Diapason of wood leaving out nine of ye Basses.

For painting the Escutchions about the loft to Jo: Dauis of Worcester — 11 — 00 — 00

381 . 2 . 8

GENTLEMAN OF THE CHAPEL ROYAL

In 1621 Thomas Tomkins was appointed one of the Organists of the Chapel Royal, junior to the famous Orlando Gibbons. Before this he had been appointed a Gentleman extraordinary of the Chapel Royal. When studying with William Byrd when he was teenager, Thomas may well have already been associated in some way with the Chapel Royal. The Chapel Royal was not a place, but a group of musicians at the beck and call of the Monarch. It involved having to attend His Majesty when required, usually in London. For Thomas Tomkins, living in Worcester, each trip to London involved an expedition of at least seven days. It is no great surprise that the standard of music at Worcester suffered from his frequent absences.

Thomas was already a musician on the national stage. In 1612 he wrote an anthem for the funeral of Prince Henry, King James I eldest son. Arthur Lake, the Dean of Worcester provided the words:

"Great Britain mourn, let every family mourn; O family of David, O family of Levi, sorrowing for him as for thy first born, sob and sing, sigh and say: Ah, Lord, ah, his glory!".

In November 1616 one William Laud was appointed Dean of Gloucester. He wanted a new organ like Worcester and Thomas Tomkins and Thomas Dallam were consulted by the new Dean. However the appeal failed, due to a Bishop who was an inflexible Calvinist. Laud went on to become Bishop of St David's (1621), Bath and Wells (1626), London (1628) and then Archbishop of Canterbury (1633). Thomas Tomkins became a friend and supporter of William Laud, and in 1635 the Archbishop made a Visitation to Worcester. Thomas Tomkins' son Nathaniel, who had become a Canon of Worcester in 1629, aged 30, was an enthusiastic Laudian and was greatly at odds with the mainly Puritan businessmen of the City. You could write a book on the disputes between the Laudian clergy and the Puritan Aldermen of the City.

In 1619 Thomas wrote a book of madrigals, the 26th was dedicated to his half brother John, on his appointment as Organist at St Paul's Cathedral, London. The words may be significant. Was he feeling the provincial bumpkin?

"Woe is me! That I am constrained to dwell with Mesech and to have my habitation among the tents of Kedar".

The poet Phineas Fletcher (1582 – 1650) became a close friend of both John and Thomas. Thomas also found a supporter in William Herbert, 3rd Earl of Pembroke, after whom Pembroke College, Oxford, was named. In 1625 Thomas wrote an anthem for the funeral of King James I, and the next year another anthem for the coronation of King Charles I.

THOMAS AND ALICE – CITIZENS AND BENEFACTORS.

In 1627 life changed for Thomas and Alice. Thomas' father Thomas senior, and his step mother Anne both died at Gloucester. Details of the will are not very clear, but it would seem that Thomas and Alice were financially secure – his Cathedral stipend, money from the Chapel Royal, extra money from the coronation music and patronage from the earl of Pembroke and money from his parents' will all added up. Thomas leased land from the Dean and Chapter on College Green, on the south side of the Cathedral, and built a new house. The house is still there today, only slightly altered and now occupied by the Headmaster of the King's School (9 College Green). The property is described as having a "hall, kitchen, buttery, 5 chambers (above stairs), a garrett and a high turret or study on the third floor, and the garden included a water pump, woodhouse and coalhouse." Other sources suggest that the study doubled up as an observatory, much in vogue at the time. Thomas now received rent from his old house, and the Song School remained in the old house.

In the same year he built the house Thomas endowed a major Charity. Thomas "delivered unto the Maior, Alderman and Cittizens of the Cytty of Worcester, the some of fifty pownds to bee lent unto two younge Trades men of the said Cytty That are yong beginners in their trades, whereof Clothiers before others are to bee preferred And the said Two yonge men Are from tyme to tyme for ever by the Chamber and Common Councell of the said Cytty to be elected." Every two years the City Council was to choose two young men, to be given £25 each to set them up in business. After two years they were to start to pay back the loan, at the rate of 20 shillings (£1) a year, to pay it back not to Thomas Tomkins but to the Mayor and Aldermen, for them to distribute 10s a year to four aged and honest devout people in need. We know that the charity remained intact until 1642, by which time Thomas and Alice would have given £400, benefiting 16 young Trades men, and 28 aged and honest devout poor folk would be receiving 10 shillings per annum. (It is difficult to calculate equivalent 2012 prices, but the young Trades people would have received at least £20,000 each, Thomas and Alice would have given at least £320,000 over 15 years, and the poor folk would be receiving at least £75 per annum.)

If Thomas was most involved with the Charity, Alice was very much involved in practical acts of charity in the community. The Churchwardens' accounts of St Michael in Bedwardine, close to the Cathedral, reveal that in 1616 John Heekes wife died, leaving two small children. The family was poor and "hade received alms and bread money on several occasions." Alice made a waistcoat for one of the children and took a turn in fostering one of the children. We know from John Toy's sermon at her funeral (2nd February, 1642) the sort of good neighbour she was. He said: "She bred up orphans, sent often meat, and money to sick neighbours, her servant hath been seen to distribute good pieces of money to many poor families from year to year, from house to house. I am sure if it were known who sent it, it was the servant's fault, for she charged her the contrary."

And she and Thomas were equally generous to their own family. Thomas' half brother John, who had become Organist at St Paul's Cathedral, London, died in 1638, closely followed by his wife Margaret. With no hesitation Thomas and Alice took care of John and Margaret's three children: John, aged 7, Sylvanus, aged 3, and Thomas, less than a year old. John and Sylvanus became King's scholars and gained places in the cathedral choir, leaving traces of their studies at Thomas's side, by scribbling their signatures in one of his autograph manuscripts. Thomas was too young. By the time he was old enough to be a Chorister, there was no choir.

The house built by Thomas Tomkins in 1627, in which he lived until 1654

CIVIL WAR

Life was about to change radically for Thomas, both in his personal life, and also in his professional life, both here at Worcester and as a member of the Chapel Royal. On January 29th, 1642 Alice died, aged 78. In the same year King Charles I set up his standard at Nottingham on 22nd August, marking the beginning of the Civil War. Fighting soon spread to Warwickshire and Worcestershire. On September 16th Sir John Byron and his dragoons took Worcester for the Crown. It was a temporary victory as on September 24th the Parliamentary army arrived in Worcester, having marched from London, and occupied the city. And to quote William Dugdale, writing later in the 17th century:

"When the whole (Parliamentary) army, under the command of the Earl of Essex, came to Worcester, the first thing they there did, was the prophanation of the cathedral, destroying the organ; breaking in pieces divers beautiful windows, wherein the foundation of that church was lively historified with painted glass, and barbarously defacing divers fair monuments of the dead." He goes on to describe the horses and soldiers in the side aisles and quire, and concludes: "Also, to make their wickedness the more complete, they rifled the library, with the records and evidences of the church; tore in pieces the Bibles and Service-books pertaining to the quire; putting the surplices and other vestments upon their dragooners, who rode about the streets with them."

Despite this account, somehow the Dallam Organ was not completely wrecked. Valentine Green, in a book published in 1796, describes how one of the organ's attackers apparently lost his footing, fell from the screen and broke his neck. I guess his friends became nervous or superstitious and the organ was not completely wrecked. When the Parliamentary army moved on after a few weeks, and the Royalist troops re-occupied the city, the organ was restored and survived for almost another four years.

However, for Thomas there was only a short respite. On the morning of 29th May, 1643 a Parliamentary force of 3,000 men and eight cannon, made an unsuccessful attempt to capture the city. The main attack was in the Castle area, the area now occupied by the King's School. Thomas's house on College Green was right in the firing line, and his house was hit by a "cannon shotte". The main damage was to the high turret and study at the top of the house, where Thomas had his study, which doubled up as an observatory. Many valuable manuscripts were lost. Thomas made his protest in a verse anthem, taking as his text the opening of Psalm 79: "O God, the heathen are come into thine inheritance: thy holy temple have they defiled, and made Jerusalem a heap of stones." More than a bit of poetic licence and exaggeration, but nevertheless leaving the family homeless for a few weeks. The Cathedral records show that the repairs cost 4s 4d, paid on September 13th "To the Mason for tiles, lime and work done in reparation of Mr Organist's house, ruined by cannon shot."

About this time a widow named Martha Browne began to play an important part in Thomas's life. Her husband had died in October 1641, leaving her with two sons aged 8 and 5 years. Nathaniel, the elder boy was a chorister, for whom Thomas was responsible for 'teaching, keeping, dieting, apparelling, ordering and lodging'. The young widow and the ageing widower married sometime in the mid 1640's. Both were alone, and both responsible for bringing up young children, and Martha needed security for herself and her two boys.

Meanwhile the Royalists did their best to strengthen the city's defences against any more Parliamentary attacks, which were bound to come sooner or later. The Parliamentary army turned its attentions on Worcester again in May 1646. The Cannon bombardment of the city began on 11th June. Seeing the writing on the wall Thomas got together some friends on July 20th and removed parts of the Dallam Organ, and hid them, possibly in his own house. Three days later, after Evening Prayer at 6 p.m., and after receiving a Blessing from the Bishop the city's leaders went to Rainbow Hill and formally surrendered to the Parliamentary forces. Several Regiments of Foot then occupied the city. What remained of the organ was torn out and burnt. Thomas, with the Dean, Canons and Bishop was homeless, jobless and almost penniless. The following day, after the final service in the Cathedral, Hugh Peters, Cromwell's Chaplain preached in the Cathedral.

It would appear that Thomas may well have been given accommodation of some sort in the village of Shelsley Beauchamp, on the banks of the River Teme in the west of the County. If he did not live there, it seems that many of his household goods were taken there for safekeeping. In Worcester he had no organ. There were no services, certainly not involving music or a choir. In the words of his biographer Anthony Boden:

"Thomas' world had been shattered, and he would have been all too sadly aware that he was one of the last representatives of an artistic golden age. He looked out upon a bleak, occupied cityscape, the cathedral silent and locked, his life's work seemingly as much in ruins as the city around him."

This was enough to break the will of any man, let alone someone aged 75 years. But not Thomas. No longer able to provide music for the Church, he returned to composing keyboard music that had served to lift his spirits at different times in his life. His thoughts went back to those whom he had known and counted as friends. In October 1647 he wrote the 'Pavan: Earl Strafford', remembering the Earl of Strafford, adviser to King Charles I, who had been executed 6 years previously on May 12th 1641. Also, later in 1647 he wrote the 'Pavan: The Lord Canterbury', in memory of his great friend and supporter Archbishop Laud, who was executed on 10th January, 1645. It was almost exactly 30 years earlier he had advised Laud, then Dean of Gloucester, about a new organ for Gloucester Cathedral. And then, on February 14th, 1649, just 15 days after King Charles I execution, Thomas wrote the 'Sad Pavan: For these distracted times', in memory of King Charles I, his employer at the Chapel Royal for more than 23 years.

While all this was happening to Thomas, Parliamentary Clergy were living in the Canons' houses. In 1647 the Bell Tower was demolished and sold. The lead and oak beams fetched £617. 4s. 2d. The Cathedral lands were also sold, in 30 lots, for £23,652. 14s. 3 and a quarter pence. (At 2012 prices we estimate £5,800,000). At some stage Thomas, with his second wife Martha, her sons, and Thomas' nephew Sylvanus were able to move back into their house on College Green. He was obliged to pay a fine to the Parliamentary Committee for the privilege of living in his own home. In 1649 Thomas was also in dispute with his neighbour about the exact nature of the lease on the neighbour's house that Thomas had built at the same time as his own house, in 1627. He was also in dispute with the Parliamentarians about land at Dodderhill, near Droitwich, which he jointly owned with his son, Nathaniel.

Nathaniel being a clergyman had all his land confiscated, and his father seems to have lost out too. On June 17th, 1650 the Mayor and Aldermen of Worcester signed a certificate, supporting Thomas. It read

"We, the Mayor and Aldermen of the City of Worcester do by these presents certify that Thomas Tomkins (late one of the Gentlemen of the late King's Chapel) being of the age of 78 years, has lived here very near 60 years. Always reputed an honest quiet peaceable man, conformable to all orders and ordinances of Parliament, and ever since the troubles began has had his constant abiding with us."

On the strength of this support from the City Elders Thomas was able to continue living is his own home on College Green. In 1650 Theodosia, the wife of his now dispossessed son Canon Nathaniel Tomkins died. It is not clear where they were living at the time.

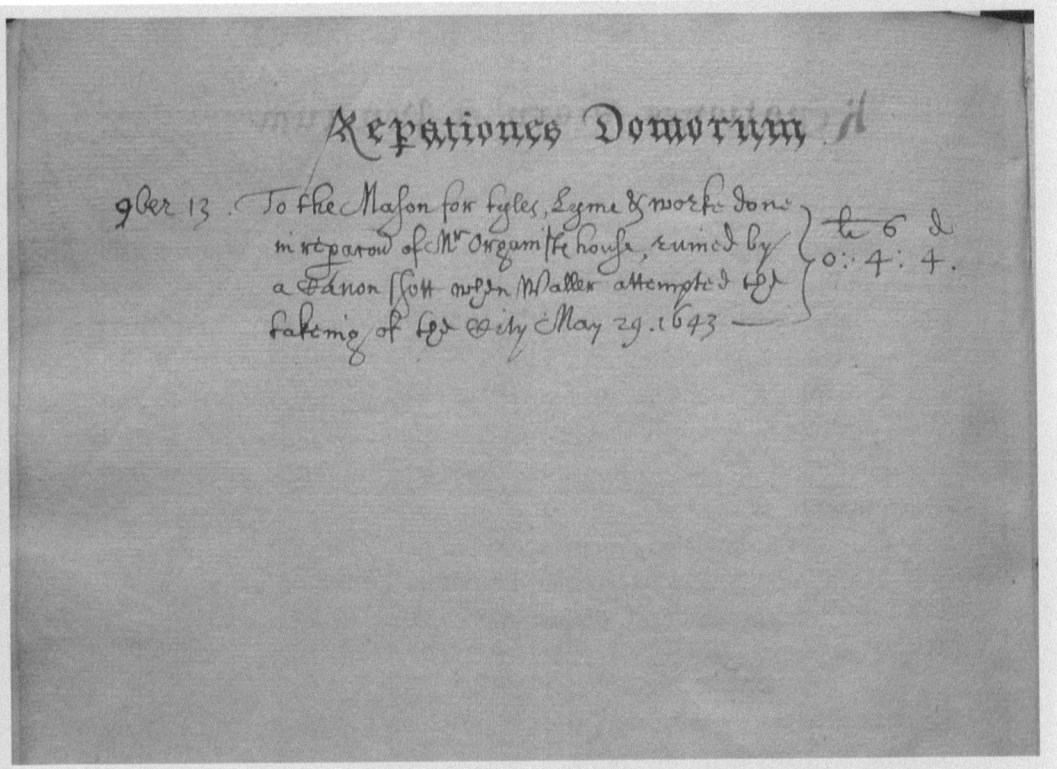

The Repair Bill for the repair of 'Cannon Shotte' damage to Thomas' house. (September 1643)

THE FINAL YEARS

1651 was a momentous year, not only for Thomas, but for the whole city, for the country, for the King and for the Parliamentarians. On August 22nd King Charles II entered the city with 11,000 Scots and 2,000 English troops. They hurriedly strengthened the city defences, especially Fort Royal outside the Sidbury Gate, but to no avail. Twelve days later Parliamentary forces, numbering 25,000 men under the command of Oliver Cromwell, re-took the city. 3,000 Scots were killed, other prisoners were slaughtered in ambushes, 400 houses were destroyed, one fifth of the city's housing stock. King Charles II fled, eventually to the Continent. It must have been a traumatic time for all living in the city.

We know that Thomas was in serious financial difficulties, forced to endure greatly reduced circumstances. In May, 1651, he owed money to the "tailor, smith, mason, shoemaker and mercer" as well as private individuals. Interestingly he still made provision for the poor in his accounts, "Ten shillings to the Poor". In 1653 his second wife Martha died. Thomas had already given up composing. In the same year Oliver Cromwell declared himself Lord Protector.

But there was yet one more twist in the saga of Thomas. In 1654 his dispossessed son Nathaniel, widowed in 1650, married a widow, Mrs Isabel Hall. She was the daughter of Guthlake Ffoliott, at one time Clerk to the Dean and Chapter. She had been married three times, and by her first husband had inherited the Manor at Martin Husingtree. She and Nathaniel Tomkins set up home there and invited Thomas to join them. He was to spend his last two years there in comparative luxury and quiet. And it sparked him into composing more music. Now into his eighties he wrote the 'Galliard: the Lady Ffoliott', in honour of his new daughter-in-law. Sad Pavans were put behind him. The music was once again very upbeat. He wrote 'Perpetual Round', a piece of great virtuosity for Virginal, and keyboard variations on a popular gallows song 'Fortune My Foe'.

Thomas died and was buried in the Churchyard at Martin Husingtree on June 9th, 1656, at the age of 84.

POSTMORTEM

Our story is not yet complete.

First, after the Restoration of the Monarchy, services restarted at Worcester Cathedral on the 31st August, 1660. By Easter 1661 a Choir had been formed. In August of the same year Giles Tomkins, the second son of Thomas Tomkins' half brother Giles, who was still organist at Salisbury Cathedral, was appointed Organist. Thomas' son, Canon Nathaniel Tomkins was restored as a Residentiary Canon of the Cathedral. Plans were made for a new Organ. In 1662 Thomas Harris made plans, and after an abortive re-build by William Hathaway in 1663, Thomas Harris of London was awarded the contract for the new organ. The specification was so much like Thomas' beloved Dallam Organ of 1613, with a few additions. Was Harris making use of parts of the Dallam Organ that Thomas had hidden in his house three days before the city fell to the Parliamentarian Army in 1646? It could well be, because Worcester Cathedral's Receiver General's Book for 1661 - 1662 seems to show that a Mr John Tomkins sold an organ to the Dean and Chapter for £40. John Tomkins, Thomas' nephew had inherited his house and possessions, which may well have included significant parts of the 1613 organ hidden by his uncle. I like to think that significant parts of Thomas' Dallam organ were restored at the same time as the Restoration of the Monarchy, and Thomas Tomkins' work lived on after the Restoration in a very tangible way.

Overleaf: *The Receiver General's Book, showing the purchase of an Organ from Thomas' nephew John Tomkins (1661 - 2)*

Dr Dowdeswels 27. 7s exscribed No. 22. 1662
        Exceptios
The Deans Heriot for 1660 — 06 – 00 – 00   moneys owing to ye Church
  Received Heriot yt annu sed — 05 – 00 – 00
To be discounted for Baggs & pac- } 00 – 3 – 4   To mr Tomkins ——— 55ᵗ – 18ˢ – 1ᵈ
  sing entred in a great Booke   Dr Dowdeswell ——— 86 – 06 – 4
Organ being in ordr ——— 40 – 0 – 0   mr Oley ——————— 99 – 10 – 1
mr Tomk: to ye allow of 3ˢ bad money — 1 – 0 – 0   mr Glen ——————— 113 – 1 – 9
To discount mr Deans bursary   Dr Arston ————— 117 – 15 – 1
  Fees and 1661. Domus. 16 – 6 – 8   Jo Barlow ————— 200 – 10 – 1
To discount in Compoto in decano   mr Reignolds ——— 106 – 13 – 9
  anno 1661. 25ᵗ – 19ˢ – 0   mr Wm Thornburgh – 26 – 10 – 9

In mr Tomkins Acc in decano   Dr Crofts his stall owes the Church
  Epistles & Heriots – 5 – 1 – 6 }   Dr Crowthers
  Coursing Heriot — 6 – 0 – 0   } 27 – 8 – 2   over payd ——— 90ᵗ – 3ˢ – 3ᵈ
    Fees — 16 – 6 – 8   }   mr Giles Thornburgh }
must be taken out of mr Tomkins   is over pd & owes } 5 – 8 – 11
  Exordace to xx vis his debt to   mr Tomkins in }
  Dean Oliver ——————   pay exceptions } 4 – 12 – 5

mr Tomkins is to pay 4 – 12 – 6ᵈ   This above said sum & 2ᵗ more
  & Clear all Accts   being Allowed him for the
                                                     Charge & Damage in Removeing
                                                     the Organ He is to allow for
                                                     it ——————— 38ᵗ

This above written was ye Drs pay.
 & added No. 21. 1665.
mr Giles Thornburgh Received of mr Thornhill pt of
 His Rents Ten pounds & stopped it in his Acct this
   Day: So mr Giles Thornburgh owes the Church more
 Then above say ———————————— x li
       mr Owen owes Quilletts (got of him pd him
           at Audit 1665.) to mr Giles Thornburgh.

Secondly his work still lives on today, in the shape of so much music that has survived. This was largely due to Canon Nathaniel Tomkins, his son. Denis Stevens wrote in his biography: "Nathaniel knew that his bounden duty was to create an imperishable musical memorial to his father's skill and piety". In 1668 Nathaniel published 'Musica Deo sacra', and so insured that a large number of his father's compositions for Church choirs would survive for centuries to come. 'Musica Deo sacra' contains 5 services, 5 psalm tunes, Preces, 2 Proper Psalms and 94 anthems. There are a further 2 evening services, 2 psalm tunes, 2 litanies, 1 responses and 18 anthems that have survived the ravages of time, mainly in Cathedral and University Libraries up and down the land. There are also 65 pieces for Keyboard, 25 pieces of Saecular vocal music and 34 pieces for a musical Consort that have survived to this day. The illegitimate son of a Vicar Choral of St David's Cathedral, and his housemaid, had come a long way, through one of the most turbulent times in the history of our nation. He still lives on in the musical legacy we have received from his genius.

Overleaf: *The title page of the one of the original Volumes of 'Musica Do Sacra', published by Thomas' son Nathaniel in 1668*

BASSVS.

MUSICA
DEO SACRA
&
Ecclesiæ Anglicanæ:
OR,
MUSICK
DEDICATED
To the HONOR and SERVICE of GOD,
AND
To the Use of CATHEDRAL and other
CHURCHES of ENGLAND,
Especially
Of the CHAPPEL-ROYAL of
KING *CHARLES* the First.

By
THOMAS TOMKINS.

LONDON.
Printed by *William Godbid* in *Little Britain*, and are to be
sold by *Timothy Garthwait* in Little S. *Bartholomews* Hospital.
MDCLXVIII.

BIBLIOGRAPHY

Boden, Anthony
(2005)

Thomas Tomkins. The Last Elizabethan.

Burney, Charles
(1776 - 1789)

A General History of Music (4 volumes)

Butcher, Vernon
(1981)

The Organs and Music of Worcester Cathedral

Dugdale, William
(1681)

A Short View of the Late Troubles in England

Green, Valentine
(1764)

A Survey of the City of Worcester

Green, Valentine
(1796)

History and Antiquities of the City and Suburbs of Worcester

Habington, Thomas
(1639)

A Survey of Worcestershire

Noake, J
(1866)

A Survey of Worcestershire

Rimbault, Edward
(1872)

The Old Cheque Book or Book of Remembrance of the Chapel Royal

Stevens, Denis
(1957/1967)

Thomas Tomkins 1572 - 1656

A Sermon at the Funeral of Mrs. Alice Tomkins (British Library E154)

Diary of Henry Townshend of Elmley Lovett
(1640 - 1643)

DOCUMENTS IN WORCESTER CATHEDRAL LIBRARY REFERED TO IN THE TEXT

1613	Dallam Organ List of Donors	D248
1627	Lease of Buildings on Palace Green	A 7: 10
1642	Repair of Dallam Organ	A 26: 23
1643	Repair of Canon Shotte	A 28: 66
1661	Restoration Organ - George Dallam	A 73
1661 - 62	Receiver General's Book	A 125: 3 & D 508
1663	Treasurer's Accounts. Payment to William Hathaway	A 26
1664	Harris paid £400 for Restoration Organ	D 250
1664	Details of Restoration Organ	D 251

www.ingramcontent.com/pod-product-compliance
Ingram Content Group UK Ltd.
Pitfield, Milton Keynes, MK11 3LW, UK
UKHW041959230426
12048UKWH00008B/422